**Investing Basics**

presents:

# Options Trading Successfully for Beginners

## (w/ FREE BONUSES)

## *Making Money with Options in just a FEW HOURS!*

## F.R. Commerce

## *3rd Edition*

**Special thanks to:**

The Investing Basics Team

The Stock Market Investing Association

Options Trading Group

OPTIONS TRADING

The Investing Club

Business and Investors Association

and many more people who have helped
contribute to this work

BONUS: Successful Forex Trading

Copyright Notice

Disclaimer:

# Introduction

A lot of people are afraid to try options trading. They feel that it is so complex that only scientists can understand it. they shy away from it because they feel that options trading is some subject that is too hard for anyone, let alone a person who has no experience in the subject of investing

But, there's no need to be so hesitant.

Because the basics of option trading are easy to understand - there's a good learning experience here that helps those who need the guidance.

First, you may not realize it, but you can essentially control the underlying assets - the stock, bond, or other commodity within the option contract - within the given time frame. You have the "option" (no pun intended) to buy, sell, hand over the rights, or just hold on to them. Did the stock price suddenly skyrocket? Imagine buying that same stock for a really low price. Did the stock price suddenly drop? Imagine selling that same stock at the original price. Your choices are virtually endless.

Next, Some investors prefer buying options instead of the underlying asset because the former is cheaper to buy than the latter. Furthermore, they can control the number of shares for a lesser price.

The first two parts introduce you to the world of options. They differentiate between stocks themselves and the options bound to them. They also show you how options work and all the terms options use.

The next parts will send you into the fire: you will be armed with various strategies, as well as do's and don'ts as you start your options campaign.

If you feel more than confident enough to take on the real world of options, try your hand on the real money online exchanges - and trade your way into victory.

Congratulations again for buying my book. Now press on to victory.

# PART I: What Options Are & How They Work

# Chapter 1: Options Explained

There are so many investment vehicles available to everyone. Investors can have bonds, stocks, and mutual funds. They can also try options trading if they have already gained skill and expertise in investing. Options are popular because they are versatile. Depending on the risk appetite of the investor, options trading can be conservative or speculative. As such, the investor has the power to protect and control his/her position if the index or the market moves.

## What are Options?

An option is actually just an agreement that the buyer has the right to transact (right to buy or sell) the underlying asset at a predetermined price at a particular date. This means that you will be getting the stock for that price, instead of a different price as the stocks fluctuate. It is commonly an agreement between two parties for 100 stocks of a company. As a form of security, an option binds the buyer and seller into a contract with strict properties and terms.

Let's say I want to buy McDonald's stocks (NYSE MCD) sometime later. The stock price is currently at $101 per share. However, they seem to be doing well at the moment and the stock price might go up. I decide to have a call option; a contract that gives me purchasing rights to McDonald's Stocks. I want to buy 10 shares of the stock at $101 exactly 60 days from now. I have the option, and I wait.

Now fast forward 55 days from now.

Let's say McDonald's stocks rose to $200 per share. I have the "option to buy 10 shares of McDonalds stocks at $101 each".

Well, if the stock has risen to $200 per share, of course I would; imagine the discount!

On the other hand, let's say McDonald's stocks fell to $50 per share. I have the "option to buy 10 shares of McDonalds stocks at $101 each". Well, if the stock has fallen to $50 per share, using my "option" would be a terrible idea. I would just let the option contract expire and buy the stock at $50 per share instead.

You might think there is more to it, but in a way, you've probably been doing this before. If you've ever bought insurance for yourself, your car, your home, or even your family, this is similar in nature to it. Options trading is similar in this way. When you buy a new car, you get insurance on it in case if something happens to it. You don't know how much the repairs might be on that car if something happens, nor do you know the price of a car as time goes on. It will increase, but the insurance will help protect you. Options trading is the same way. With the example above, you might notice that the price of stock rises up to 200. Instead of spending $20,000 on new stock, if you're buying it with options trading at $101 a stock, then you'll be getting it at almost half the price. Once you buy that, you can then sell and trade at any time in order to make more money. With options trading, you're looking at what the best investment is for your money, and then moving on from there once you find something that's worth the price you want to pay.

It's a way to help you get a stock at a great price when you can, and if you're not happy with the price of it now, you can wait for the option to expire before you buy stock in that company.

## Why Learn Options?

Investors must take the time to study options trading because it can be a good diversification strategy to include options in their portfolio. Options are used by huge multinational corporations as a hedging strategy against the risk of heavily fluctuating stock prices, such as forex fluctuations. They are also offered to the best employees by corporations which want to retain them.

It also increases a leverage in your pay. simply put, many companies want their investors to have a better foothold before trusting stock in the person. Options trading will show you have the upper hand in this. It also enables you to have a larger payout when you decide to sell stock.

It also makes your portfolio look better as well. If you're new to options trading, you can get into this easily, and your portfolio will end up looking better than many who have been in the business for a longer period of time.

**Options Difficulty Level:**

Although options trading can be versatile, it is sometimes very risky and difficult. Most of the time, brokers warn that options aren't for everyone. They also warn that investors should be careful about investing their capital because the risk of loss is great. Investors who aren't knowledgeable about this type of investment usually try other investment vehicles instead.

Are you scared? If not, read on.

Lack of knowledge isn't a hindrance to options trading because investors can learn about it. If investors aren't into speculative trading, they can still invest in options through conservative trading. There are so many resource materials and references that investors can read to learn about options and how they are traded. You can also look at the stock market and have a better feel for it as you continue on. It might seem like a terrible idea right now, but if you taked it slow and work with the system, you will get a feel for it.

Having a good grasp on what options trading is how you get started.This chapter gave you the basic definition of options trading, and what it is at its basic level. As you read on, you'll get into the nitty-gritty on what options trading is, and how to do it.

# Chapter 2a: Why Trade Options?

The first thing you might ask yourself is why you would options trade. Well first of all, you might do this to protect yourself. If the risk is great, you might do this in order to get a great deal. It also helps you control where your money is going as well. You do have to be careful though, because if you're not watching the market, it can backfire on you. There are different means of trading options however, and this chapter will go over why you should employ trade options when investing.

## Hedging and Speculation

Investors dabble into options trading due to hedging and speculation. These two means are what you should learn first before going into trade options, and it explains how you approach trading options when they surface.

Hedging is when you protect yourself against anything bad happening. It doesn't mean that the bad event isn't going to happen, it just protects you if things do go bad and you are at risk of losing money. The investors who employ hedging use different instruments in order to protect themselves against anything bad from happening with their money. Hedging insures an investment against any event which may cause the price to fall. In other words, it's like using a 'safeguard' against losing value. Large corporations use options as a form of hedging. There are also retail investors who take advantage of hedging.

On the other hand, there are experts who advise not to use options as a hedging strategy if the investor doesn't know the underlying asset well enough - because in this case, the investor will surely fail. For example, if the person is hedging too much and buying insurance on something they don't know, they could be losing money instead of taking the risk and increasing their profits. However, done properly, hedging is a great strategy to limit losses.

There are also investors who trade options as a speculative strategy. Options allow investors to profit in 3 ways: when the price goes up, when the price goes down, or when the price moves sideways (meaning, the price stays still or goes up and down within a range). A lot of profit can be made from speculative activities. Speculating can be done by examining the market, determining the trends, and figuring out where to go from there. If you're familiar with the market, this might be the way to go.

However, options trading for speculation can be quite risky. An investor who wants to profit from options trading, as a speculator, must be able to correctly determine: the direction of the asset price (will the price rise or fall?); the movement's timing (when will the price change?); and the price movement's magnitude (the price will change by how much?). It's also important to notice any patterns when it comes to speculation, but make sure that you don't rely on just that in order to help you determine your next move. It's like strategizing an attack in the military, but there is always a risk in it.

Although options trading is risky, a lot of investors at least dabble in it - because of leveraging and other advantages options offer.

## Advantages And Disadvantages Of Options Trading

Even though options trading is complicated, a lot of investors are doing it. They can profit with the price movement of an underlying asset without actually investing in the asset.

Also, It is actually cheaper to invest in options than in the actual asset. Options trading takes huge advantage of leveraging (you'll learn this later). It is essentially having WAY more access to resources than what you originally have. Using options as leverage, investors can receive huge profits - even if the price moved a little in the right direction.

This means that the investor can earn more money per actual invested dollar. Options trading offers limited risk - except when written puts or calls are uncovered. An investor can only lose as much as the premium he/she has actually paid.  If you don't put everything into it, you're not going to lose everything.this is good if you want to dabble in taking a risk, but aren't ready to go full-out and jump into things.

With options trading as well, another advantage is you can use hedging to prevent any risks from becoming too high. If you don't put calls on your options trading, you're at low risk. You can also use hedging to protect yourself from serious fluctuations in the market. when you start off, it's imperative that you work in this manner.

Another advantage is that you can make money even when the stock isn't making money. Because of the option to trade up, down, or sideways, you have many ways to increase the leverage that you want when you're trading. many times, even if the stock is falling, you still can come out in the black at the end of it.

The commissions are a lot less as well. If you go through an online broker service, you can get these options at a low price due to the competition of it. You can also reduce the risk of losing money, and you won't have to worry about commissions becominga problem in the market.

Furthermore, options trading is versatile. It allows investors - and especially day traders -

to react accordingly depending on where the price moves. You also can invest in many markets, and it's not limited to only a couple of options. From agriculture to foreign currency, you have many options when you decide to invest in trading options. You dont' have to worry about just going with a company such as a major corporation, but you can invest in other places and still make a profit off of this.

And finally, a great benefit is the speed of investment. As soon as the stock rises, you get your profit, and then you can trade it for other stocks and make more money. the speed of the market allows you to work fast, and because of it, you'll end up making more money than you ever dreamed of.

On the other hand, a lot of options are short-term investments only. An investor can lose money in a few months if he/she makes an incorrect prediction. Some investors shy away from options trading; often they want to invest in long-term investments.

The commission rates can also become a bit of a problem as well. Sometimes the commission rates are so high, they go take at least 30% of what you made. You'll end up losing a chunk of your money, so you should watch out before you put your money into something.

Another disadvantage is taxes. Yes, they are present in what you're dealing with. Taxes are put on everything, except in very rare circumstances. You should make sure to fill out an IRA form and keep tabs on taxes before you start investing your money. having a cushion for taxes will help you in case if something does go bad.

Furthermore, an option isn't tangible unlike a stock certificate or a certificate of deposit. It doesn't provide proof of ownership - just paid rights. You won't be able to prove to people of the ownership of the stocks, unless if it is a stock certificate.

And finally, there is the problem of uncertainty. it is a bit scary investing for the first time. You don't know what you're getting into, and in turn this could cause the risks to be higher than the gains. it's important to look at what you're dealing with, how you'll go about this, and what your plan is. Be prudent when you start off in order to limit issues later on.

Stocks can be a bit scary to deal with initially, but once you have a firm grasp of what you're dealing with, the rest will fall into place.

# Chapter 2b: Options, and their Characteristics

## Parties To An Options Trade

Basically, there are 4 kinds of participants to an options trade.

For both call and put options, there are buyers and sellers for that particular stock or commodity at hand.

Holders are those who buy an option. Try not to confuse yourself with the terms. Remember that holding an option is to "have THE RIGHT to buy/sell the underlying stock". If you're "holding" an AAPL call option, you have the right to buy the option at a certain price. If you're "holding" a put option for the same stock, you have the right to sell it at a certain price.

On the other hand, Writers are those who SELL an option contract. On this end of the deal, options writers are obliged to have the underlying stock, or cash for purchase, ready for transaction. If you're "writing" an AAPL option, decide on the option type (call or put), the stock price, the expiration date, and the premium (we'll cover all this later). You're going to "give out THE RIGHT to buy/sell the underlying stock you've arranged". Oh, and don't forget to either have the cash or the stocks in hand.

In either call or put option, Holders have no obligation to either buy or sell when the contract expires. They, however, have the right to buy or sell. Writers, on the other hand, have an obligation to fulfill - based on whatever option contract terms written.

**The Call Option**

In a call option, the option holder can buy the underlying asset at an agreed date and price. A call is almost the same as "going long on a stock" - expecting the price to rise. In essence, the buyer of a call option hopes that the underlying asset will increase in price during the agreed time period.

Now you have to be careful with this. If you as a holder buys the asset at the increased price and go along with it, You could end up losing everything. There isn't a cap on it, so if it continues to increase, your losses will increase. This is the risky party of investment, and sometimes if the market is volatile, you could go from having everything to losing everything in a snap.

**The Put Option**

In a put option, the option holder can sell the underlying asset at an agreed price within a certain period. A put is the same as "going short on a stock" - expecting the price to fall. An investor holding a put option profits if the price of the underlying asset falls prior to the expiration of the contract.

This is good if you're keenon taking advantage of a rise in stock. Having that option for a moment could cause you to earn a lot of money, but when it falls, you're not penalized. If you want to make a profit quickly without being tied down to that stock forever, then this is the option to go with.

many of the people who invest in put options are bearish in the market, and they are working towards making a profit when things fall. They are watching for when stocks fall to make a move, and that's how they gain leverage.

## Option Variants

An American option can be transacted any time before the option expires, while a European option can be transacted only at the expiration time.

For long term investors, there are options which can be held for many years. A long-term equity anticipation security is very similar to the traditional option. However, it can be held for a number of years.

A plain vanilla option is a simple put or call option. An exotic option may be a plain vanilla variant, or a completely different option.

## Transacting Or Closing Out An Option Trade

In reality, most options are neither bought nor sold prior to the expiration of the contract. A lot of investors don't exercise their options. Sometimes, option holders sell away their options, while some writers buy back and/or hold their own options.

In reality, 30% of these options, in this case, become expired and worthless while 60% are closed out or traded out. Only 10% of options are actually exercised.

And this is fine; sometimes, the option's value itself can prove profitable enough for you to trade away.

## How Options Are Priced

Options prices are based on the "premium" calculated for them. The premium of an option is actually its intrinsic value plus its duration-based Time value. A common way to compare this is to an insurance premium, which is what you pay for the option. With options trading, this is what you pay for the option that you will be buying and the stock you'll be getting. We'll discuss this in later chapters...

# Chapter 3: Comparing Options V.S. Stocks

Remember that an option is just a contract; the options holder has the right to either buy or sell an underlying asset at a particular price before the expiration of the contract.

In most cases, a stock is chosen as an underlying asset of an option. Other underlying assets can be commodities, foreign currencies, government securities, exchange-traded funds, and stock indices. In many options exchanges, a stock option is usually equivalent to 100 shares of stock of a particular company.

An option contract must have the following:

- expiration date

- strike price

- number of shares / commodity quantity

- underlying asset

- option type: call or put, along with any variants

A stock option is often preferred because it has limited risk, as well as having the possibility to earn more money through leveraging. An option investor can only lose up to the total price he/she paid. This is possible because an option contract has an expiration date. If the buyer doesn't exercise his option, he just loses his initial cost to get the option. But, the option seller doesn't have the same advantage.

A stock option permits an investor to set the price for a certain time. It is relatively cheaper than buying the stock. Furthermore, an investor can earn more money from options trading through leveraging.

**Options and Leveraging, for example:**

Let's say an investor purchased 100 shares of a particular company stock at $100 each. Therefore, it has cost him $10,000. However, he also has five $200 premium call options each with a $100/share strike price, which will allow him the right to purchase 500 shares as well.

If after 1 month the share price rose to $110, the gain on his stocks is $1,000. However, what if the option premium for the same stock also increases - to $300 for each whole contract?. For the regular stock investment, the gain is 10%; for his stock option values, the gain is 50%.

But for ALL the underlying stocks within his five options, he can exercise all the options, buying 500 more originally at $50,00 overall, then SELLING them back at $55,000 - that's a $5,000 profit.

Leveraging has its disadvantages, too. If the price didn't move to the right direction, the percentage lost is magnified.

Using the same example, if the share price fell to $80 ($10 lower than the option's strike price), the loss is 20%. On the other hand, the option premium might decrease to $80, or a 60% percentage loss overall.

As such, an investor must exercise caution in using leveraging when trading options. They should have a good prediction on the market and the stock before investing in it. they should also be looking at the company and see how their profits are at that present moment before taking the time to invest in a stock.

**Time Frame**

A regular stock has no expiration date. It means that the stockholder can hold onto his stocks indefinitely. On the other hand, a stock option has an expiration date. An out-of-the-money (unprofitable) option only becomes worthless when it is not exercised prior to its expiration date.

## Ownership

Ownership of a share of stock is proven by a certificate issued by the company. A stock option doesn't have a certificate of ownership; whoever holds it owns it. With the option though, there is no paper for it, you just get the option.

## Volume

A company can only issue a fixed number of shares. Therefore, investors can only trade a limited number of shares. It is commonly only 100 shares for each stock option

On the other hand, there is no limit as to the number of stock options investors can buy or sell. However, a stock option doesn't offer dividends, voting rights, or ownership of the company if the option isn't exercised.

## Market Exchanges

Professional traders, individual investors, and institutions trade options on an options exchange. It is possible for an entity to transact a lot of options contracts at the same time.

Like regular stocks, a stock option is traded on a market regulated by SEC. Brokers facilitate the options transactions just like the regular stocks. Monitoring transactions and performances are easily done through their respective marketplaces.

# PART II: Some Important

# Terms

# Chapter 4: Remember These Options Terms

## Strike Price

The strike price is the value of the underlying asset that can be sold or bought whenever an investor exercises the option. This affects the moneyness of the option, and it is the major determining factor in the option's premium when it comes to how much it'll go for.

This means that if the underlying asset is a stock, and if it's a call option, the stock price must be higher than the strike price in order to generate a profit. If it's a put option, the stock price must be lower than the strike price in order to create profit. The option can't be exercised if the conditions aren't met prior to the expiry of the contract. A listed option is traded on an options exchange like the CBOE or Chicago Board Options Exchange. It has a fixed expiration date and strike price.

**Listed Option**

A listed option is equivalent to 100 shares of stock. A call option is "in-the-money" (meaning, it's profitable) if the current market price of the underlying asset itself is higher than the strike price.

On the other hand, a put option is "in-the-money" if the price of the asset is lower than the strike price. The intrinsic value is the amount by which the option became in-the-money.

**Premium**

The premium is the total price of the option. Factors affecting the premium include volatility, time value, strike price, and price of the underlying asset. It is usually difficult to compute for the option premium, but not with a good pricing model to follow (more on this on a later chapter). However, the premium is often the asset's intrinsic, plus the time value.

It is basically the price the option buyer needs to pay the option seller when they buy the option. It is the risk that's associated with it, and it can be a small amount or a large amount. It also is determined by the volatility fo the market as well, and if the stock carried a higher risk, the premium will increase. This is similar to insurance, for if there is a higher risk because you've been in accidents or have had many medical issues, the premium will increase as a result of this.

The intrinsic value is defined as the 'in-the-money amount' - or the strike price, if it's a call option.

Time value, on the other hand, is probability that the value of the option will increase. For example, if the premium is $9.25, the intrinsic value may be $9 while the time value is $0.25.

In most cases, options are traded more than their intrinsic value.

**Conversion**

A conversion is created when a call option is sold, a put option is bought, or at least 2 options have the same expiration and strike price. It is commonly done when the options are overpriced comparedto the existing stock. Doing this allows you to gain a riskless profit as a result, and if you see something like this, you then take advantage of it.

A delta is the change in the price of an option while an exercise is a decision to transact the option brought about by the right provided in the contract. This is commonly used when the market shifts and the prices change on something. An expiration is the date when the contract will terminate. This means that the option is no longer valid and is gone. The grantor is an entity or person who is ready to exercise the option prior to the expiration of the contract. The stock option expires on the third Friday of the expiration month.

**Intrinsic Value**

The intrinsic value is the price of the option upon immediate exercise. An option is said to be out-of-the-money if it doesn't have intrinsic value.

A strangle is a position which involves the buying of both call and put options with different strike prices but similar expiration. The time value is a component of the premium in excess of the intrinsic value.

**Underlying Asset**

An underlying asset is a form of security that the option seller has. It's an obligation to deliver to purchase from the option holder in the event the option is exercised. This is some shares in a specific company in this case.

These options are usually also available in currencies, indicies, and commodities as well.

These basic terms are what you need to know when it comes to experiencing options trading in the stock market.   knowing these basic terms will put you on the right path to success.

# Chapter 5: Options Pricing & Trading

A lot of people find options trading difficult to understand. This is primarily because it is difficult to understand all of its parts.

However, once people understand the science behind options trading, they can eventually harness its art form in order to meet their investment goals. The price of an option is highly dependent on the price of the underlying asset, the volatility of the asset, as well as the remaining time prior to the expiration of the contract. This chapter will go over how the option's price and trade works, and what it means at the core.

## The Asset's Price

But at the core, the price of the underlying asset is important in option pricing. It's what everything is based off of, and it's the price of the asset. It is what will determine the put and call options as well, and it's what you will be looking at to invest in.

In essence, when the asset price increases, call option prices also increase. However, the put option prices decrease.

On the other hand, if the asset price decreases, then the opposite happens. The put option prices increase and the call option prices decrease. This is to ensure that whatever way it does go the put and call options follow.If the asset will only be important for a short period of time, commonly people exercise a put option on it. But, if the asset has potential, a call option can be put on it as well.

Because options expire, time is important in option pricing. The longer the expiration time, the higher the option price. As time moves towards expiration, the option price decreases. That's why it's important to see the immediate gains from it, because an option price may decrease over time, and you might not get the stock for that price ever again.

## Volatility

Volatility is also a factor in option pricing. In the case of stocks, those which are stable have lower option prices than those stocks which are extremely volatile. There is also such a thing as implied volatility, which is based on the belief of the market maker. If a lot of people invest in a particular stock, its price will go up. The market maker can adjust the implied volatility to increase the option premium.

As a versatile investment, an option is a cheaper alternative to a stock. Options trading can offer more profits through leveraging. It also limits overall risk. You won't be putting all of your money into one thing, in hopes that it won't fall. Plus, because an option is only valid until the expiration date, your money won't be tied up in it forever.

An investor can only lose money up to the option premium only - essentially what they paid for the option in the first place. Unless if there is a call on it, they won't lose anything else with the option besides the premium, which might be a small price to pay in the case of a stock. Therefore, margin requirements are not required if the investor wants to buy an option.

On the other hand, the option writer must buy or sell the underlying asset if the holder exercised his option. An options writer can keep the option holder's premium money paid

- but only if the holder failed to buy or sell the underlying asset before the contract expires. As such, a margin requirement is needed in the part of the writer.

## Theoretical Value Of An Option

A theoretical value is different from an option premium. As has been discussed earlier, an option premium is paid by the next option holder so that he /she may buy or sell the underlying asset before the option contract expires.

The theoretical value is just an estimate of the present value of the option. It is computed based on the formula of the chosen pricing model. It includes factors like timing prior to expiry, strike price, and price of the underlying asset. Because of the changes these factors undergo during the lifetime of the option, the theoretical value fluctuates continuously until the option expires.

A theoretical value is generated through an option pricing model. Every factor has a certain value and forms part of the theoretical value at a future time. If the stock is chosen as the underlying asset, its theoretical value includes implied volatility, which is based on the option's supply and demand. An investor uses different pricing models to know the option's theoretical value.

Variables like implied volatility, timing, strike price, and underlying asset price are part of the computation. A theoretical value changes over time because these variables also change. A lot of investors and traders use this theoretical value to know the option's value and risk in order for them to make an intelligent decision. Trading platforms also offer updated values while pricing calculators can also be used online.

Using a theoretical formula to determine how much you can potentially make off of an option or stock is important when you're starting out. Using this formula will help give you a good idea of what you'll be getting ou tof this, and because of it, it'll help you determine whether or not investing in that option is worth it.

Knowing the basics of how stocks work, the assets, and what happens to them, you can manipulate the market and get the most for the money that you put into it.

# Chapter 6: Options Pricing Models

Here are a few pricing models to follow when trying to figure out an option's price. You just have to DEEPLY understand a few good models, and then use a calculator online. This chapter will go over some of the basic models out there, along with how you can understand them.

### The Black-Scholes Model

In 1973, Robert Merton, Myron Scholes, and Fischer Black introduced the Black-Scholes pricing model as a way of computing option premium. Since then, this model has become the most popular. In fact, Merton and Scholes received a Nobel Prize in

Economics two years after Black died in 1995. Black, however, was still acknowledged for his role although he wasn't given the Nobel Prize because the Nobel is awarded to living persons only.

The Black-Scholes model is applicable only to European options, both call and put, and doesn't include paid dividends in its calculation. However, it can still be used by using the ex-dividend value of the asset.

The model assumes that the option can only be exercised at the time it expires. And that's why only European options are considered. Furthermore, aside from not considering paid dividends, this model also doesn't take into consideration any commissions.

It also assumes that the market is efficient and that the movements in the market aren't predictable. Volatility and risk-free interest rates are constant and known.

Lastly, the Black-Scholes model assumes that returns are distributed normally.

This option only takes into consideration one risky asset, such as a stock, and then a riskless asset, such as cash. with this, there is no arbitrage opportunity, but there is a way for someone to borrow money at a riskless rate with this model. You can also buy any stock with this model, even a fraction of it, without any hidden fees or costs. With this option, the derivatives are determined at the current moment, and the payoff as well. You can create a long stock investment with a short option investment.

To compute for the option value, the Black-Scholes model requires the following: - risk-free interest rate

- implied volatility

- timing (expressed as a percentage of the year)

- strike price

- and the current price of the underlying asset.

The mathematical formula is complicated. An average person may be intimidated to use it. Fortunately, there are options calculators available online which can be used to compute for the price using this model. Furthermore, there are analysis tools provided by trading platforms which be used to compute for the price.

This is a good way to get an approximation of the investment, but it's not the only think you should be relying on. due to the volatility of the market, liquidity risks, and sudden changes and risks, it could cause you to expose yourself to some major risks. There are also extreme price changes, and most of the time, money does not come with an unchanging value in the real world. It's a good way to geta feel for what you're about to do, but at the same time, you shouldn't rely completely on this.

## The Cox-Rubinstein Binomial Option Pricing Model

A variation of the Black-Scholes model, the Cox-Ross-Rubenstein model was developed by Mark Edward Rubenstein, Stephen Ross, and Carrington Cox. The primary advantage of this model is that it uses a lattice-based model and takes into consideration the price movement of the underlying asset over time. A lattice-based model considers the changes in different variables over the life of the option. Therefore, it results to a more accurate option price. It looks similar to a tree, and it progresses in that manner to the expiration of the stock.

This model is used for American options. It assumes that everyone is indifferent to risk so the returns are equivalent to the risk-free interest rate.

The Cox-Ross-Rubenstein model further assumes that arbitrage isn't possible because the market is perfectly efficient. The price of the underlying asset can never go up and down simultaneously. It can only go in one direction at any given time. Different points in time can be specified during the life of the option. Because of this, it is possible to create a binomial tree.

Normally, it's calculated from the beginning of the option to the end of it, and then back again. Once that's done, it's then calculated with the factors of the changes in dividend prices, along with the changes in option prices. All of this is calculated together and put into a theoretical model to help others understand where their money will be going.

The biggest advantage to this, is that it works for American stocks. another benefit, is that it also helps you see exactly where a stock is at a specific point. You can take a look at this, and through the analytic properties of it, you'll know where that stock will be approximately in the future. it's helpful in that regard.

The biggest limitation however, is that it takes forever to calculate. you're examining a ton of numbers all at the same time, and many of the older computers can't do it. With the changes in technology however, software is able to keep up with the speed of changing numbers. It's advisable that you get an online calculator in order to see where a stock will be at a certain point of time.

Like the Cox-Ross-Rubenstein model, online pricing calculators and analysis tools provided by trading platforms can be used to know the option price.

**The Put/Call Parity**

As a pricing concept, the put/call parity was introduced by Hans Stoll in 1969. According to his study, there is a relationship between the European call and put options with similar strike price and expiration date.

It means that, for every call option value at a particular strike price, there's a corresponding put option value for it. The same goes for put option values. There's a corresponding call option value for a put option value at a specific strike price. The relationship exists because a position is created, which is the same position as the underlying asset when there's a combination of put and call options.

The returns must be similar for the underlying asset and option so that arbitrage won't arise. Traders and investors who take advantage of arbitrage can make a profit if the opportunity arises.

The put/call parity is used to test pricing models for European options. If the result of the pricing model doesn't satisfy the parity check, it means that arbitrage can occur and the model must be rejected as a pricing strategy. There are several ways to compute for the put/call parity.

Luckily, some trading platforms offer analysis tools. These provide visualizations of the put/call parity.

But of course, you don't have to fully memorize all the pricing models. Just pick one suitable for your situation, have an online pricing model calculator handy, and let the numbers move for you.

# PART III: Let's Start

# Investing!

# BONUS Chapter: Employee Stock Options

Although not very common, an employee stock option is used by some employers to entice the best employees to work in their company. It is used to keep promising employees and great talent from leaving the company.

This option is nearly the same as other stock options. The employee may buy the company stock but he/she is under no obligation to do so. An employee stock option binds the employee and employer to the details of the contract. On the other hand, the regular option binds 2 unrelated parties to a contract.

Employees can also invest in options. However, not all employees have the opportunity to do so because the employer usually offers it to the best employees. Also, not all employers offer the stock option.

However, if managed properly, it can be a lucrative investment. If an employee is offered a stock option, that employee should see to it that he/she understands the ins and outs of this stock option - in order to generate the maximum benefit.

It is important for employees with stock options to understand how it affects personal income. Employees must also understand the taxation of stock options and its nature.

An employee can buy a pre-set number of company shares at a pre-determined price within a pre-determined time.

**Employee Stock Option Types**

A stock option can be classified as incentive or non-qualified.

A non-qualified stock option is offered by the employer to consultants, outside directors, and non-managerial employees. A non-qualified option has no special tax treatment.

An incentive stock option, on the other hand, is strictly offered to executives of the company. The incentive stock option has favorable federal tax treatment because it qualifies under some certain provisions in the Internal Revenue Code.

Both stock options are difficult to implement because they have to follow specific guidelines set by the employer and the IRS.

## Exercise Timing

At the onset, the employees don't fully own the stock options. They have to follow a vesting schedule. The schedule starts at the day of granting the options. Depending on the terms of the contract, the employees can exercise the options on certain dates.

In most cases, only a number of shares can be exercised per vesting date. At the end of the contract, the employees can no longer buy company shares. The exercise price is the amount of money the employees will have to pay for a share of the company stock. It is also the basis for computing tax payable and gain. The gain is computed as the difference between the market price and the exercise price.

**Taxing:**

A non-qualified employee stock option is taxed when it is exercised. The gain is treated as compensation and forms part of the taxable income. If the shares are immediately sold by the employee, it will be short-term capital gain and will be taxable using the regular income tax rates. If the shares are sold after a year, it will be part of the long-term capital gain and the tax payable will be reduced.

The incentive employee stock option is not taxable when exercised. The gain, however, may be an alternative minimum amount. If the employee sells the shares within a year after the options were exercised, the gain will form part of ordinary income. The gain will be considered as long-term capital gain if the shares are kept for at least a year after exercise and sold at least 2 years after the date of grant.

# Chapter 7: The Process

Now that you know the basics of how to buy stock options, it's time to learn the process of doing so. Stock option buying might seem like a crazy ordeal, but the truth is, it's not. this chapter will go over the process of how to buy stock options, and what to do when you do.

**Remember..**

Investors must realize that when they buy options, they are just taking advantage of the profit potential within the certain time frame. They don't buy the stock itself. Also, options decrease in value when they're held for a long time. That means that once you have it, it's important that you use it as soon as you can.

Recall that a call option provides the holder only the right to buy a predetermined number of shares of the underlying asset at the strike price as long as it isn't expired yet. A put option, on the other hand, is only a right to sell a fixed number of shares of the asset at a predetermined price within a certain period of time. It may sound repetitive; but for newcomers, it's important to understand the difference between the two.

An investor must first decide the kind of underlying asset to invest in. He/she must also determine the price direction of that asset. This is where you should be looking first. figuring out what to invest in is key. many times, you have to do an analysis of the market at hand and see the trends that are being made with a stock. If the stock isn't doing well, then don't look into investing it. Instead, move onto something else that has a better chance at being successful.

You should also start with products that aren't volatile. In a volatile stock, it could go from great to poor within a day or so. Those types of stocks are hard to control, and it could set you up for losses. Instead, of with a stock option that's less volatile, but still has the chance of being profitable if you do invest in it.

Hint: Most investors opt for index exchange-traded funds as their underlying asset because ETFs are more consistent and less volatile.

## Charting

Charting software can be used to draw resistance and support lines while indicators can be used to find out the price direction of the asset. There are also different chart models to help you determine where the price will go, and thesewill be discussed further in the following pages.

## Bear or Bull spread?

The next step is to choose either a bull put or a bear call spread, based on either resistance levels or support levels. This will determine how the stock otpion si spread, and what will happen if you do choose to invest in it.

A resistance or support level is a certain price range or limit where an asset's price has difficulty reaching. Thus, it's an uncommon price an asset can reach. Once an asset's price reaches a resistance level, it will usually revert back to original prices.

A resistance level is usually a high price limit, while a support level is usually a low price limit.

Stop losses are also placed below the support level or above the resistance level. As the name implies, they're designed to 'stop losses' during your trades.

A bear call spread is used with resistance levels. It contains calls with the same expiration, but with different strikes attached to it. The objective of the bear call spread is to maintain a bearish or neutral underlying asset. This strategy depends on the profitability of a premium before it retires. This spread takes into consideration that it will fall below what the original price was, and the stock will end up being lower. In other words, you would EXPECT the asset's price to plateau or fall. This option requires that you must have already bought the outlay to determine where it will go. Where it eventually ends up isn't completely known at first, but it's a good way to see how the payout will be as the stock option starts to fall. The most you get out of this is the premium amount, and the most you can lose is the amount until the long-call caps at that amount specified, so it's important to be mindful when doing a bear-call spread

On the other hand, the bull put spread is used with support levels. It is done with a short and a long put, with the long being less than the short. this allows the investor to get some of his money back, and is profitable when the market starts to move. It has limited risk and potential, and the most that the person can earn is the premium plus whatever trend the stock decides to rise. The most that you can lose with this is when the long put is capped, but most of the time there is lower risk. With this though, it does take a bit more of a prediction on where this stock will eventually get to. You should know those numbers when you start in order to determine where the profit margins will eventually end up being. The goal of the bull put spread is for the underlying asset to stay bullish or neutral. In other words, you would EXPECT the asset's price to plateau or rise.

It is important to decide at what price a spread will be set. In most cases, the price for a bear call spread is placed above the resistance level. The price of the bull put spread, however, is placed below the support level.

**Potential Profit/Loss**

It is possible to compute for the profit/loss potential manually. However, a broker usually provides tools which investors can use to compute for it.

In general, the spread difference times 100 less the profit is considered as the risk exposure of the investor:

*Risk Exposure = [ ( |Sell posn. - Buy Posn.| ) x 100] - profit*

In order for risk to be justified, it is best to ensure there is enough profit.

It is also possible to compute for the danger zones and break even points through probability calculators. It is advised for investors to maintain a specific success probability and never disregard it in exchange of a better profit.

The spread can be placed between the sell and buy positions near the price of the underlying asset. For example, the investor can sell a $140 call option and purchase the $141 call option for a bear call spread. On the other hand, the investor can also sell a $125 put option and buy the $124 put option for a bull put spread.

$1 losses based on the option prices aren't a big deal - compared to the opportunity of huge, leveraged profits once prices go the correct way.

**Price Monitoring**

It is important for the investor to monitor the price movements daily. If the price of the underlying asset goes in the correct direction, the holding investor can let the option expire. On the contrary, the investor can buy back the sold option at a loss but retain the option; it can increase in value until it makes a profit or breaks even. That's why many watch the stocks like a hawk in order to determine when a person should buy into the option they have, or if they should wait for the opportune moment. Missing one day could change everything.

Furthermore, the investor can close the position by trading out any time he/she makes a profit. If you do make a profit from this, then it's best that you get out now before the market changes. At the beginning, you should take all of your wins as a chance to get out before you lose everything,and as you become mroe familiar with what you're doing, you will know when it's best to get out and when you should stay in with the stock.

# Chapter 8: Managing Options

## How To Hold & Buy with Options

Buying options don't guarantee that the buyer will exercise them prior to expiration. There are, actually, 3 ways to use options.

First, the investor can hold the option to maturity then buy the underlying asset at the agreed price before it expires. Investors do this when the current market price if the asset has gone higher than the strike price.

Second, the investor simply exercises the option sometime before it expires. This is done when the price of the asset fluctuates up and down the agreed price. If the investor believes that the price won't go any higher, he/she can exercise the option immediately after registering a higher price than the strike price.

Lastly, the investor can let the option expire. Investors do this if the price of the underlying asset continuously decline. The loss the investors experience is limited only to the option premium.

**How To Sell with Options**

Unlike holders, option writers must sell or buy the underlying asset if the holder decides to exercise it. They must buy or sell the asset at the strike price within the agreed contract period - even if the market price of the asset is higher or lower than the agreed price.

A covered call allows the writer/seller to sell the underlying asset which he/she owns. The call writer must sell the asset at the agreed price if the buyer exercises the option. This allows the writer to get all the benefits of the stock as well as the dividends as well. The only time this doesn't apply is when there is an agreement for the person to share the shares that are earned with the stock.

from this though, there is still the issue of the person not fully benefiting from this. They did get the premium and dividend back, but they opted out of any other potential risings in the market, so you should be careful before going into this.

An uncovered call, on the other hand, allows the seller to sell the asset which he/she doesn't own at the start of the contract. The seller stands to lose a lot of money if the price of the underlying asset has risen sharply and the buyer decides to exercise the option. This means that the investor has to buy the asset at a high price only to sell it a loss to the buyer. This can cause a significant loss as a result of the trade, and it can make the person lose a lot of money in the investment as a result.

**Watch the Market...**

It is a common observation that traders allow their options to expire. This is true for traders who trade long positions. The market needs to reach a price to make the option profitable. If a trader wants to consider an option, he/she must look into the probability that the market will reach a certain price. A cheap premium doesn't guarantee a good trade. A good market and potential for that means that it will be a good trade.

You should watch the market for a certain period of time when you are looking into buying a stock option. See the pattern of it, and see if there is a chance for profit with that. If there is, then it's time to go for it. If not, then it might be best to sit that one out and not take the risk with it. You can watch the market by checking the stocks every day and seeing which ones are doing good, and which ones to stay away from.

**The Average Monthly Range**

A lot of options traders prefer looking at the option premium rather than the possible returns. Although it is important, they tend to focus too much on it, thereby missing the possibility that that the market may reach and eventually exceed the strike price.

In most cases, it is best to keep options trading simple. To decide whether an option is a good trade or not, the options trader can calculate the market's average monthly range. It is a number which offers perspective on the volatility and the possibility of reaching break-even point.

The average monthly range can be compared to other stocks average ranges as well. You might see a stock that has a good trade option, but the average range is terrible and there isn't a chance for profit. However, let's say you see one that's a bit higher than the other, but you notice that there is a lot of potential for that stock. It's better to go with the latter, because it can mean a potential increase in your own profits, and it will end up benefitting you more as a result later on.

## Using The Average Monthly Range

To compute for the average monthly range, the trader needs historical prices.

If the stock is chosen as the underlying asset, it is possible to retrieve historical high, low, open, and close prices within a certain period.

The average monthly range needs the daily high and low values of a certain stock.

The average price can easily be computed during the time the market fluctuates between the high and low of a given month. In most cases, conservative traders use the monthly open and close values. The low price is subtracted from the high price during the month to get the range, which is then added up and divided by the months.

[month 1: high price  - low price ]

+ [month 2: high price - low price] + …

/ (number of months)

(Note: use a spreadsheet or specific calculator/analyzer for this!)

In general, a trader can consider doubling the length of the position to come up with the time frame. Then, it is broken up into 2 time blocks.

Be careful though. This strategy isn't helpful when the implied stock volatility makes the premiums unreasonable. Smaller traders will be forced to buy at out-of-the-money strike prices because they don't have enough capital. The average monthly range will tell traders to skip the option trade or use a debit spread strategy in order to be close to the present market price.

The average monthly range can be used in any market at any given time. However, it mustn't be used alone. Market directional analysis must also be used. This concept only prevents options traders from buying cheap premiums with far-out-of-the-money which offer limited returns.

**Debit Spread**

In a debit spread, an investor buys a higher-premium option and sells a lower-premium option.

Example:

| Trader, Bull: | S t o c k F@$10 | | | |
|---|---|---|---|---|
| | | | | |
| Buy: | C a l l : $ 9 / stock | Stock F | 100 | P r e m : $120 |

| Write +Sell: | Call: $11/ stock | Stock F | 100 | Prem: $90 |
|---|---|---|---|---|
|  |  |  |  |  |
|  |  |  |  |  |

| Trader, Bear: | Stock F@$10 |  |  |  |
|---|---|---|---|---|
|  |  |  |  |  |
| Buy: | Put: $11/ stock | Stock F | 100 | Prem: $120 |
| Write +Sell: | Put: $9/ stock | Stock F | 100 | Prem: $90 |
|  |  |  |  |  |
|  |  |  |  |  |

A good benefit of the debit spread is that it offers option traders limited risks and a possibility to get nearer to the present market price instead of purchasing the option outright. The break-even point may also be lower than purchasing an out-of-the-money option.

Furthermore, the investors limit their gains in outright option and must be content with a maximum, defined gain. Under some market conditions, this trade may have a favorable trade-off. It will also keep traders grounded on what the market can do.

The promise of unlimited gains is only true when the market moves historically. This is very seldom. Investors who trade for capital appreciation won't stay long if this kind of speculation is observed.

# Chapter 9: Basic Options Trading Strategies

A lot of investors and traders lose money in options trading because they trade options without understanding its ins and outs first.

A solid strategy is needed to profit from the trade. It allows a person to maximize the profit and mitigate the risk. It takes only a small effort to learn how to make use of the power of options and its flexibility.

## The Covered Call

The covered call strategy allows an investor to buy the underlying asset outright. Then, the investor must write and sell a call option immediately after the purchase on that same asset. The number of shares must be equal.

Example:

| Trader: | | | | |
|---|---|---|---|---|
| Buy: | | Stock A | 100 | $10 ea. |
| Write +Sell: | Put: $ 1 0 / stock | Stock A | 100 | Prem: $100 |
| | | | | |
| Profit So Far: | $100 | | | |

This strategy is used by investors for their short-term trade and when they have neutral opinion on the underlying asset. It is also used by those traders who want to protect their investment against any possible decline in value. It's a good basic strategy to start out with, and if you're worriedabout lsoing out on a psossible investment, then this is the way to go.

**The Married Put**

The married put strategy is used when investors are bullish about the price of an underlying asset. They buy shares of the asset outright, and then buy a put option simultaneously of the same number of shares. They do this to protect their investment against possible losses on a short term. It's a way to cash on an investment at the moment, but they don't have to worry about losing anything when the going gets tough. the potential for gains in this is unlimited in a sense.

The married put strategy is like an insurance which determines a floor price in case there's a dramatic plunge in the price of the asset.

Example:

| Trader: | | | | |
|---|---|---|---|---|
| Buy: | | Stock A | 100 | $10 ea. |
| | Put: $10 / stock | Stock A | 100 | Prem: $100 |
| | | | | |
| Cost: | $100 | | | |

## The Bull Call Spread

The bull call spread strategy is used when investors are bullish over a particular asset and they expect the price of the underlying asset to rise moderately.

They buy a call option at a certain strike price then simultaneously write and sell a call option at a higher price. When prompted, the trader essentially buys the lower-priced asset, then simultaneously sells the higher-priced asset - thus, generating profit.

For this strategy to work, both call options must have the same underlying asset and expiration month.

Example:

| Trader: | | | | |
|---|---|---|---|---|
| Buy: | C a l l : $ 1 0 / stock | Stock B | 100 | P r e m : $100 |
| Write + Sell: | C a l l : $ 1 3 / stock | Stock B | 100 | P r e m : $100 |
| | | | | |
| | | | | |

## The Bear Put Spread

The bear put spread strategy is used when investors are bearish about the price of an underlying asset. In this case, they expect the price to further decline.

They buy a put option at a particular price, then write and sell another put option at a price lower than their first option. When prompted, the trader essentially sells the higher-priced asset, then simultaneously re-buys the lower-priced asset - thus, generating profit as well.

Like the bull call spread, this will only be successful if investors transact the same asset with similar date of expiration. This strategy limits both profit and, more importantly, loss.

Example:

| Trader: | | | | |
|---|---|---|---|---|
| Buy: | P u t : $ 1 0 / stock | Stock C | 100 | P r e m : $100 |
| Write + Sell: | P u t : $ 7 / stock | Stock C | 100 | P r e m : $100 |
| | | | | |

|  |  |  |  |  |
| --- | --- | --- | --- | --- |

## The Protective Collar

The protective collar strategy locks in profit without the need to sell the shares of the underlying asset. Investors buy an out-of-the-money put option, then write and sell an out-of-the-money call option. Again, this only works if investors transact with the same asset.

It used by investors who go long in an underlying asset and have earned profits from it. If the asset price drops, the held Put option will secure profits. If the asset price rises, you secure profit once someone exercises your written call option.

Example:

| Trader: | S t o c k D@$12 |  |  |  |
| --- | --- | --- | --- | --- |
|  |  |  |  |  |

| Buy: | Put: $10 / stock | Stock D | 100 | Prem: $100 |
|---|---|---|---|---|
| Write + Sell: | Call: $14 / stock | Stock D | 100 | Prem: $100 |

# Chapter 10: Common Options Trading Strategies

### The Long Straddle

The long straddle strategy is primarily used to limit losses and maintain gains. In this case, the loss is limited only to the price of the options.

To be successful, investors must buy a put and a call option at the same price, the same expiration date, and the same underlying asset. They use this strategy when they believe that the price of the asset will move drastically. However, they're not sure of the direction the price will take.

Example:

| Trader: | Stock E@$10 | | | |
|---------|-------------|---------|-----|-----------|
| | | | | |
| Buy: | Put: $10 / stock | Stock E | 100 | Prem: $100 |
| | Call: $10 / stock | Stock E | 100 | Prem: $100 |

## The Long Strangle

The long strangle (not to be confused with the previous one) strategy is a cheaper strategy than the long straddle because the the options are bought out-of-the-money. It is used to limit losses to the price of the put and call options. Furthermore, investors employ this strategy when they believe that the price of the underlying asset will move significantly. However, they don't know which direction the price will move.

To be successful, investors buy both a put and a call option with the same asset and same expiry date, but the prices of the options differ from each other. The strike price of the put option must be below the call option's strike price. This way, the options will both result to out-of-the-money.

Example:

| Trader: | Stock F@$10 | | | |
|---------|-------------|---------|-----|------------|
| | | | | |
| Buy: | Put: $9 / stock | Stock F | 100 | Prem: $100 |
| | Call: $12 / stock | Stock F | 100 | Prem: $100 |

## The Butterfly Spread

The butterfly spread strategy is a combination of the bear spread and the bull spread strategies. It also uses various prices. A kind of butterfly spread strategy allows investors to buy a call option at the lowest strike price. Then they simultaneously write and sell 2 call options at a higher price and another call option at the highest possible price. So if someone exercises your written option, you promptly exercise yours. You end up selling high and buying low - thus inducing profit.

It is also possible for them to purchase a put option at the highest price then simultaneously write and sell 2 put options at a lower strike price while selling the last put option at the lowest strike price. So if someone exercises your written option, you promptly exercise yours. You again end up selling high and buying low - thus inducing profit again.

Example:

| Trader A: | Stock G@$10 | | | |
|---|---|---|---|---|
| | | | | |
| Buy: | Call: $10/ stock | Stock G | 100 | Prem: $100 |
| Write +Sell: | Call: $13/ stock | Stock G | 100 | Prem: $100 |
| | Call: $14/ stock | Stock G | 100 | Prem: $100 |
| | Call: $16/ stock | Stock G | 100 | Prem: $100 |

| Trader B: | Stock G@$10 | | | |
|---|---|---|---|---|
| | | | | |

| Buy: | Put: $10/stock | Stock G | 100 | Prem: $100 |
|---|---|---|---|---|
| Write +Sell: | Put: $8/stock | Stock G | 100 | Prem: $100 |
| | Put: $7/stock | Stock G | 100 | Prem: $100 |
| | Put: $5/stock | Stock G | 100 | Prem: $100 |

## The Iron Condor

The Iron Condor strategy is difficult to implement. It's not for new options investors because it requires a lot of time and practice to be successful with it. Investors have both a short and long position in 2 kinds of strangle strategies: a bearish and a bullish direction.

But no matter which direction, if someone exercises your written option, you promptly exercise yours. Done correctly, you end up selling high and buying low - thus inducing profit again.

When using this option technique, try not to confuse the strike prices. You should always end up buying lower and selling higher.

| Trader: | Stock H@$10 | | | |
|---|---|---|---|---|
| | | | | |
| Write +Sell: | Put: $ 9 / stock | Stock H | 100 | Prem: $100 |
| Buy: | Put: $ 8 / stock | Stock H | 100 | Prem: $100 |

| Write | Call: | Stock | 100 | Prem: |
| +Sell: | $ 1 2 / | H | | $100 |
| | stock | | | |
| Buy: | Call: | Stock | 100 | Prem: |
| | $ 1 4 / | H | | $100 |
| | stock | | | |

## The Iron Butterfly

The Iron Butterfly combines a short or long straddle with a strangle. It is somewhat the same as the butterfly spread. However, the difference is that the iron butterfly uses a put and a call option simultaneously. This strategy limits losses and gains within a certain range. Investors ensure costs are minimized and risk is limited by using out-of-the-money options.

| Trade r: | Stock I @ $10 | | | | |
|---|---|---|---|---|---|
| | | | | | |
| Buy: | Put: $9 / stock | Stock I | 100 | Prem: $100 | Out of the money |
| Write +Sell: | Put: $11/ stock | Stock I | 100 | Prem: $100 | In the money |
| Write +Sell: | Call: $9 / stock | Stock I | 100 | Prem: $100 | In the money |
| Buy: | Call: $12/ stock | Stock I | 100 | Prem: $100 | Out of the money |

**The Synthetic Long call Strategy**

This is a strategy used when two methods of spreading are used with another long call strategy. For example, if you used a married long call with a bear call, this would be a synthetic long call. The purpose of this, is to create two long calls of the same nature. It can help you gain more revenue in the long run,and there are advantages to this. One thing to keep in mind though, is to make sure tht you're not doing anything too risky with each all. Determine if the call is worth it, and then act after that. Knowing what the risks are is how you'll be successful with the synthetic longcall.

**Collar Call**

A collar call is when you use underlying stock along with protective puts and selling call options. You use the puts and the selling call against the underlying stock. the purpose of this, is because they are out-of-money options, and from this, it's similar to the out-of-money covered call. It is used in order to gain premiums on options, without risking the potential loss in the long-term due to the drop of price or the reduced risk of security.

All of these options strategies will help you understand where you're going with this, and from there, you can determine the path of where your own strategies will go. it's an important to know where everything will end up falling, because many times people don't realize the true nature of various calls, and knowing the spreads and potential strategies will help you manipulate the market better and achieve better results.

# Chapter 11: Avoiding Mistakes in Options Trading

For new options trader, it is advisable to learn several strategies and improve on making solid returns over time. There are also different things you should keep in mind before you begin options trading. there are mistakes that can be made, but if you're careful and avoid the pitfalls, you will succeed with this.

**Don't begin by purchasing out-of-the-money call options.**

A lot of experienced stock traders who moved to options trading often use this strategy: purchase a call option and wait to see if it will make a profit. This is similar to the "buy low, sell high" strategy in stock trading. While it may provide handsome profits in stock trading, this strategy doesn't consistently provide profits in options trading. In the long run, an options trader may lose a lot of money. Also, he may discover that he's not learning anything new.

An out-of-the-money option is a cheap investment because the price depends on the probability that it will reach or get past the strike price. In most cases, that probability is low. Thus, the price of the option is also low.

A new options trader should instead write & sell an out-of-the-money call option on the underlying asset he/she currently owns. When the call option is sold, the option writer has to sell the asset. Because of this obligation, the writer can make a profit from the option. If the investor is bullish about the asset, he/she can earn some money - ready to sell the stock even as the price rises before the option expires. Don't buy right away, but instead sell and write call options in order to gain a profit as a result.

**Watch the Timing**

In stock trading, it seems difficult to predict how the price of a stock will move. The same is true with options trading. many times, the fluctuation can happen overnight, before you even know of it. The option might skyrocket in price, and becaue of that, you have to watch for any changes in the market.

A trader must usually predict correctly the direction of the price movement. They might not be accurate at first, but being able to see the difference will save you so many headaches, and you will know approximately where the options trade is going as a result of this.

However, he/she must also predict the right time the price will move in the expected direction.

If a trader with a call option makes a mistake in any or both parameters, he/she will take a loss on the premium paid. If the underlying asset takes a long time to move to the expected direction, the profit becomes smaller as the expiration date approaches. That's why, you should know where it's going to happen, and the approximate timing of the existence of the direction of a stock. See where it will fall, and from there, you can determine where you're going to end up as a result of this.

## Try Covered Calls

There's really nothing risky about selling options using the covered call strategy.

The risk lies in the ownership of the underlying asset; an investor can lose an amount equal to the difference between the prevailing market price of the underlying asset and the option's premium.

In most cases, the loss can be substantial. There is no capital risk in the writing and sale of the option. However, there is opportunity risk because the investor has a limited upside. It is possible for the buyer to exercise the option when the underlying asset's price soars. As such, the seller loses potential gain. On the other hand, because the underlying asset is owned by the seller, the price of the asset must have risen to the option's strike price.

On a flat market, the writer/seller maintains the long position while receiving the option premium. If the writer wants out after the price of the asset has gone down, he/she can actually purchase back the option in order to close the short position. Furthermore, the writer can sell the underlying asset to close out the long position. He/she may experience losses by closing the position. The sale of covered call is a low-risk and smart strategy for new option traders. An options trader can use it as he/she becomes more familiar with option trading.

**Don't use an "all-purpose" strategy for every market condition.**

The flexibility of options trading allows traders and investors to dabble into trading during all market conditions. They can do so if they make an effort to learn other strategies. They can buy spreads on various market conditions.

However, there's actually a right market condition to use it. A long spread position has two possibilities: the sale of the lower-cost option and the purchase of a higher-cost option. These options only differ in the strike price. A long call spread is a bullish position (thinking the asset's price will rise) while a long put spread is bearish (thinking the asset's price will fall).

In trading a spread, the time disadvantage of one option can be a time advantage of the other. Therefore, the problem of timing is offset with spreads.

The disadvantage of spreads, however, is that the investor is limited in his upside potential. In reality, not a lot of people earn huge profits from spreads. But, the potential loss is also limited.

Strategies that might be "all-purpose" might seem like a good idea, but sometimes using that can mask the true potential of an investment. you might be making more out of one type of an investment rather than another type. many don't realize this at first, but that's because they end up seeing that they missed out on an opportunity. Try out calls for the appropriate situations, and know what you should do in each situation.

**If "MiddleMen" are Involved...**

Investors and traders must be careful about spread trading. For brokers, spread trading may pay a lot of commissions because this kind of trading involves different trades. In computing for profit/loss, they must include commissions in the equation. Lastly, they must know the risks of the transactions with commissioners, who will demand a share of the profits. Sometimes the profit loss for paying a commissioner can be up to 30%, which is a lot if you look at how much you've put in as a premium. don't rely on middlemen in order to gain a profit. You can find cheap broker sites online, but also make sure that they are a legitimate place to use, because sometimes false broker sites exist, and that could mean an even greater loss of money as a result.

**Have an exit plan before the option expires.**

Emotions have no place in options trading. To be successful in it, traders and investors must have a plan and they must commit to implement it. A good exit plan has upside and downside exits; it also has time frames for every exit. Having a plan establishes successful trading patterns and causes people not to worry.

A new options trader must know the amount of profit that will bring enough satisfaction. The trader must also know the amount of loss he or she is willing to take. The trader must know also both amounts in advance.

When the profit has been reached, the position must be cleared. The same goes with the downside goal.

**Don't "double up" to recover past losses.**

In most cases, options traders often find themselves breaking their own rules. In stock trading, it may be possible to double up in order to recover the losses. A stock investor may buy more shares when the price is low. However, this may not hold true in options trading.

Options are different from stocks. Therefore, "double up" doesn't make sense in options trading. Time decay must be considered always. Leveraging is possible in options trading. However, it can also make the trader lose heavily. It is important to cut losses and close the position in order to avoid a catastrophe.

**Be Careful with trading illiquid options.**

A liquid market is ideal for options traders because it is easy to transact when there are active sellers and buyers all the time. Also, it ensures that the next trade will be transacted at a price which is the same as the last one.

In general, there's more liquidity in the stock market than the options market because the latter offers more choices than the former. An investor who opts to trade illiquid options may pay a higher cost than the usual cost of options.

In general, it is wise to trade options with open interest at a minimum of 40 times the volume of option contracts one wants to trade. For example, if an investor wants to trade 10 lots, his or her liquidity should be at a minimum of 400 contracts. It is best to transact liquid options.

**Don't waste a lot of time to decide to buy back short options.**

An options trader must always be ready to buy back short options. Most of the time, that trader can't decide early because he/she may not like to pay commissions. The trader may think that the contract will just expire without the buyer exercising it.

Lastly, the trader may be hoping to profit even just a little from the contract. It's better to buy back the short option than to suffer the risks of being out-of-the-money. In general, the investor must buy back the short option if there's still at least 80% of the gain from the original option sale. Failure to do so will ensure losses.

**Dividend payment dates and earnings must be included in the options strategy.**

An options trader must monitor the dividend dates and earnings of the underlying asset. Option owners can't take advantage of dividends. If a large dividend has been announced, they can exercise a call option to buy the underlying asset - thus gaining the dividends.

Although early assignment is difficult to control because it's pretty random, it is best for options traders to identify any impending dividends in order not to be assigned early.

Furthermore, the earnings season increases the price of options contracts. Any news about the underlying asset can increase volatility. It is advised to trade options after the announcement of earnings had already passed.

Pending dividends increase risk of assignment. Any trader, who still wants to trade options even with a pending dividend, must learn about the ex-dividend rate.

Furthermore, the earnings season increases the price of options and volatility. Any trader who still wants to trade options during this season might want to create a spread by going long on an option and going short on another. The price of the underlying asset is usually inflated during the earnings season. As such, investors can expect that option premiums are also inflated.

**If assigned early, the options trader must know what to do.**

An options trader who writes short options must know that it is possible to be assigned. New options traders often never consider assignment. So, when it happens to them, the impact can be debilitating. A lot of new options traders may panic if their short options are assigned. In most cases, it is best to stay rational and think of the better ways to get out of the situation.

To deal with an early assignment, traders must consider it early. If not, they would often find themselves making irrational and defensive decisions.

Market psychology can be considered. Traders may weigh the pros and cons of exercising a call or put early. If they exercise a put or sell a stock, they can get cash. At times, traders will prefer cash now than wait for expiration. This means that a put option is often exercised early than a call option. However, this may not be the case if the underlying asset is set to pay dividends.

If a call is exercised, traders can buy the underlying asset now than wait for expiration. In most cases, they would rather wait. Inexperienced traders may exercise the option early if the price of the underlying asset has risen. They don't realized that they're wasting time premium if they exercise early.

**In trading a spread, don't "leg in".**

A lot of options traders, even experienced ones, learn the hard way. They take needless additional market risk. What they should do is to deal with a spread like a singular trade. Both trades must be simultaneously created. It's not possible to run a spread without achieving net credit or debit first. This is the best way to mitigate risks and implement the strategy. Take one spread at a time, and watch the market.  an unnecessary risk will kill your ability in the future to invest, and it could cause a significant loss if one is not careful with the risks and limitations of a spread.

**For neutral trades, use index options.**

Volatility resides in each stock. If the publicly-listed company makes a major unexpected press release, the price of its stock will definitely be affected for a few days. However, that single company may not be able to affect the index very much.

Options trading using indices is a good way to protect the traders against any major movement in a particular company. It is advised that traders make neutral trades based on major indices if they don't want to worry about the impact of a single news in the price of an underlying asset.

Short spreads on indices can be profitable if the market remains stagnant. Any sudden news on a particular company can have a dramatic and quick impact on the price of its shares. In most cases, the stock will trade in a new horizon as an after-effect.

On the other hand, indices move differently. They are less dramatic. More often than not, they are not affected by a single development in a company.

## Master the Spread

A short spread can include 2 positions with various strike prices. The option with the higher price is sold while the one with the lower price is bought. The two options must have the same parameters except the price. They must be both calls or both puts. Furthermore, they must have the same volume of contracts, expiry date, and underlying asset. The ill effects of timing can be minimized because one is sold and the other is bought.

An important difference between short and long spreads is that the former is constructed to be profitable when there's a similar underlying asset. As such, a short put spread can be neutral to bullish while the short calls can be neutral to bearish. Furthermore, the spreads must have at least one option trade. For brokers, it means that traders will have to pay more than one commission.

Learning and mastering each of the spreads will help you make good decisions upon investing. You'll know when to call or put a spread, and you can determine if something is worth investing into or not. many times, when one starts out, they will call on something because of the immediately potential and the increases they see. however, if they do that, and the stock crashes, they will end up losing money that they paid. It's best to put the risk fo the premium as your initial risk, and if you feel comfortable as you continue to master the spreads, you will be successful.

## Continue Learning

Options trading can be very difficult and intimidating to most people. It is possible to lose money in it, especially if the trader is the seller because he/she has an obligation to fulfill if the buyer decides to exercise the option. On the other hand, the buyer has a right, not an obligation, to exercise the option before the contract expires. To most people, especially to the inexperienced ones, this can be a scary endeavor.

However, they fail to realize that everything can be learned. They just have to spend time and effort in researching about options trading before they try to trade on their own. There is a wealth of information available about options trading. All that is needed is for an interested investor to find the information, read, then trade.

Options trading can be risky. But, it is possible to mitigate the risk by deciding correctly. A person needs to be knowledgeable about options trading before he/she can decide favorably.

## PRACTICE: Your Move: The First Steps

And now, the real world awaits.

If you are ready to invest or trade in the real world, try your hand at any of the following top online options exchanges below:

OptionsHouse:
www.optionshouse.com

TD Ameritrade:
www.tdameritrade.com

TradeKing:
www.tradeking.com

Options Xpress:
www.optionsexpress.com

Trade Monster:
www.trademonster.com

Re-read, re-read, re-read and refresh yourself with the material in the book, until options trading & your decision making feels natural to you. Remember: it's without a doubt that Options trading is one of the more challenging investment vehicles. However, done properly, options will become your best friend - netting you FAR more investment gains than you would've thought possible.

And even then, be disciplined. If your goal is financial freedom through options, follow the course until you're successful.

**IMPORTANT NOTES:**

If it's one thing about making money through investment vehicles, it's this.

The higher the risk, the higher the reward. So, if you want to gain more, you better have the guts to be willing to lose more.

So, if you want to make money within your first few hours, be well-educated. Read well, research well, and take the plunge. Rejoice if you gain, brace yourself and carry on if you lose.

Also, don't take every loss as a huge issue. lern from it, work with it, and from there, you'll end up gaining better advantages and leverage later on. It might seem like a problem now, but if you take options trading into your own hands, you will become familiar with it, and you will havea better experience as well.

And remember: if there's any investment offers out there with tag lines like "GUARANTEED RETURN ON INVESTMENT", back away. The FTC states this as illegal. By nature, almost every investment vehicle out there is somewhat volatile: while some investments gain a lot, some investments lose a lot too.

# PART V: Intermediate Risk Measurement: Delta, Gamma, Theta, Vega, Rho, Lambda

# Chapter 12: The Different Types of Immediate Risk Management

Now that you know about the different models and how you would use options trading, it's time to talk about the trends that may come about with options trading. With the changes in the market, there are different means of how the market flows. This is important to learn, because these terms are used frequently when talking about the fluctuations in the market. This chapter will go over what each of the five major definitions are, along with a couple of examples of what they do in the market when it happens in certain circumstances.

## Delta

Delta is the Greek word for change. In options trading, it means the change in the price of the underlying asset to the corresponding change in the price derivative. It's sometimes referred to as the "hedge ratio." For example, let's say that the price of an asset goes to become .8. That means forever $1 of the underlying stock increase, the call option will increase by $.80. Usually the delta increases the closer the stock gets to the expiration of the option. At the end of it, it'll approach a delta of 1.00.

An example of this in the use of options trading is if you buy a call or put option that is out of money, the option will have a delta value from 1.0—1.0. Sometimes at-the-money ones go from .5 to -.5. It is not a constant, but it is related to other risk measurements, and it will show the rate of change of delta given by the underlying. Delta is also subjected to the implied volatility, so it's not completely reliable.

With this, you can measure the net-long or the net-short of something, along with the underlying when you take into your account your portfolio of options.

## Gamma

Gamma gives you an estimate of how much the delta changes when the price moves $1. This can tell you how "stable" the delta is. If there is a big gamma, that means that the delta can start to change dramatically, for every small move. When there is a long call or a long put, you get a positive gamma. On the opposite side of the coin, short puts and calls change the gamma to a negative one. Stock never changes so it has 0 gamma.

The graph of gamma changes, just like delta. Usually it looks like a hill, with the top being right near the strike. Gamma is highest for ATM options. This means that the ATM options changes the most when the stock prices move. If you watch how the gamma changes based off the type of option, you can see the volatility. The time passing can act as a "pulling up" to the top on a graph of gamma. As the option gets towards expiration though, the gamma starts to lower, along with the volatility.

What this means is that a position with a positive gamma is good. It will generate the deltas that help move the stock if it goes up, but if it is negative, it can hurt you regardless of if it goes up or down. Gamma helps you look at the profit/loss graph of your position over a wide range of stock prices. Negative gamma positions can be risky, so it's important not to deal with them.

**Theta**

Theta shows the time decay; it is an estimate of how much an option decreases when 1 day passes and when there is no move in the stock or volatility. Theta shows how much the option whittles away in value as time goes on. It is always changing, but it shows the rate of how something changes with time. The theta for the call and put at the same strike price though is not equal. The difference between theta calls and puts depends on the cost of the stock. When the cost of the stock is positive, the theta for the call is higher than the put. When the stock is negative, the theta is lower than the put.

Long calls and long puts always have a negative theta. Short calls and puts have a positive theta. Stock however has zero theta, meaning it doesn't get eroded with time. Theta determines the difference in extrinsic value of an option with more days of expiration to one with fewer days of expiration. Long options have negative theta and short options have a positive theta. However, if the option is continuously losing value, a short option will create a positive theta and make money, but a long one will have an ability to cause money to be lost.

As time goes on, the rate of the theta increases. When it's closer to the end of the option, it starts to increase in theta, but if it's farther away, it decreases slower. That's why the value of an option needs to be taken advantage of early on, because if you don't, you won't' get your full money for it.

Theta is highest for ATM options due to the high extrinsic value, and the theta of options with higher and volatility is lower before the expiration. Gamma and theta are opposites, and if something has a high positive gamma, it will have a high negative theta. Gamma in a way is something that provides the power to make money if the stock starts to move in a significant way. Theta is what you pay for all that power though, and the longer the stock doesn't move, the more it will hurt your position.

**Vega**

Vega is not represented by a Greek letter, but it's still very important. It's an estimate of how much the theoretical value of an option when the volatility changes by 1%. The higher the volatility means higher the option prices.

A higher volatility swings the stock price, which creates a likelihood for the option to make money by the expiration.

Long calls and puts have a positive Vega, due to the change of it changing as time goes on. Stock doesn't have a Vega because it's not affected by the volatility. A positive Vega means the option position increases when the volatility increases, and it decreases when the volatility increases. Vega also can increase when the volatility increase, and it's higher options are ITM and OTM. This means that if you have an option that's changing a lot, it will have a higher Vega.

## Rho

Rho is an estimate of how much the value of an option changes when interest rates move 1%. The rho for a call and put at the same strike price and the same expiration month aren't equal. It's the least-used letter by the Greeks, and it is one of the options strategies that isn't used as much as the other. When the interest rates in an economy are stable, the chance of an option position will drop because of how low it is.

Long calls and short puts have a positive rho, but short calls and long puts have a negative rho. The reason this happens is because of the cost to hold a stock position is built in the value of an option. It has to do with the idea of an option being a substitute for the stock position. If the stock is selling for a higher interest, you will have a higher rho, and if it's more expensive to hold a stock position, the more expensive it is for the call option. But if the interest rates decrease, the values of calls increases and the value of puts decreases. A decrease in the interest rates decreases the value of calls and increases the value of the puts.

**Lambda**

Lambda is the percentage change ratio in an option contract's price, compared to the percentage change in that same option's underlying price. Lambda is one of the Greeks that is used in derivative analysis. Lambda measures the change in an option premium for a percentage point change in its implied volatility. When the lambda is high, the price of the option will be more sensitive to the small changes in volatility. When the lambda is low, the changes in volatility will have less impact to the option's value.

Lambda is the byproduct of delta because it changes with ratio of the underlying price over the option price. Because there is a straightforward relationship with delta and not with heading, it's not very widely use. Traders prefer to use delta because it provides them with their risk profile directly. Lambda is useful to help with the selling of options to clients. The value of a lambda is around 5-15.

It is sensitive to option maturity, although quite substantially for out of money options.

All of these terms are what will help you in options trading. In the next section, we'll go over the various ways to use each of these various options strategies and how they affect the way risk management is produced. They're important to know, and it's something every options trader needs to know.

# PART VI: Intermediate Risk Management for Options Trading

# Chapter 13: Basic Techniques for Risk Management

Risk management is very important for options traders. It's something that every options trader should know, and if you don't, it can create problems later on. This chapter will go over some of the best risk management strategies for active traders in order to help prevent any snags later on when it comes to options trading. Plus, once you get these down you can use them to protect your money, and it will save you a lot of issues now, and later on.

## Why Prepare?

You might wonder why you need to learn this. First of all, it's an essential part of options trading that gets overlooked by many people. There are tons of options traders who go into it, do some trades, and end up getting great profits from this. That's great, but you can lose it all in two bad trades if you don't employ the proper risk management over time and aren't used. These simple strategies protect your profits, and they're something that every single trader should know.

**Planning Trades**

With everything in life, the first thing you must do is to plan. From wars, to even what you're going to do later on, planning and strategy is how you come out on top. It's the planning that will get you places, and successful traders plan their trades before the start any form of trading. Planning ahead is the difference between loss and failure.

Stop-loss and take-profit are two ways to help you plan ahead in options trading. A trader knows the price they are willing to pay and sell options, and they measure the return against the probability of the stock hitting the expected number. If they get enough out of it, they will trade it.

Unsuccessful traders don't even look at what they're trading, or have a plan at when they should sell in order to get a profit. They don't know how the options market is going to move, and as a result, they are like gamblers with the options they have. They might have an unlucky streak, and then emotions take over. Emotions are not part of options trading, only planning and strategy are. When there are losses, people hold on and determine that they want their money back, but then they continue to make the same mistakes. If you plan before you trade, you'll end up coming out on top of the trade.

## Stop-Loss and Take-Profit Explained

You saw above what those two words are, but you should know what they mean. It's important to have a firm grasp on this, because as a trader it can be the determining factor between you getting the sale and profit, and you not being able to.

A stop-loss is the price the trader will sell a stock and take a loss on the trade. This happens when the trade doesn't happen like they hoped. These will help to prevent the "it will come back" mentality and to limit the losses before it gets work. For example, if the stock breaks before a level, a trader will sell it as fast as possible in order to prevent losing everything.

A take profit, is the exact price a trader will sell stock in order to take a profit. It's when the option will hit the price that they want. It is when the upside is limited given the risks. If the stock is moving at a resistance level that is moving up, an options trader will sell it before the consultation takes place.

How to Set up Stop-Loss points

There are moments that you should look and set up in order to stop losses and get profits.

This is usually done with a technical analysis through formulas, but you should also look at the fundamental analysis as well.  For example, if a trader is holding a stock ahead of earnings as excitement builds, he might want to sell it off before the market hears about it. This will prevent more from investing into it, and they will get a profit off of this before it gets too risky.

Another way to do this is moving averages. This is easy to calculate and can be tracked by the market. They are usually done by a certain amount of timed averages. You can put this on a stock's chart and determine when the price has reacted and when it's at a support or resistance level.

You can also measure this and set it up is to set up treadlines. They can be made by connecting the highs and lows that occurred on a significant volume. These levels react to the treadlines and create a high volume.  You should make sure though, that use this in the long term with volatile stocks to prevent price swings that causes a stop-loss. You should adjust the averages to the price ranges you want, and the longer targets should reduce the number of signals. You should also adjust to the market's volatility. If the market isn't moving, then the stop-loss point can be tightened up. You should look at key time periods as well in order to increase stock price.

## Calculating Returns

Another way this setting up of stop and take points helps is it will help you calculate your expected return. It's important, because you can think with the rate instead of rationalizing it. It will also give you a systematic way to compare trades and sell at the most profitable time. This will give you an opportunity to see what the expected return will be. It will help determine when to trade, along with the probability of gain or loss, along with helping to make educated guess.

These risk management tools can help prevent before things get worse. It's important to know this, and it's something that every investor should take in before they start to get into options trading. This reduces the risk, and helps you come out on top.

## Chapter 14: Nine Options Trading Risk Strategies You Should Know

Partaking in options trading, there are some risk management options that can help you invest better and will make things better for you. This chapter will go over nine specific things to watch out for when options trading, and why each of these nine options are important in options trading. You should be able to use this in order to obtain consistency in options trading, along with considerable success.

### Allocation Flows Downstream

The first concept is to go over asset allocation. You should make sure that you aren't putting everything intone thing. You should make sure that you're not putting your entire investment portfolio into equities, but also into bonds, real estate, and commodities. You should also work to make sure that the diversification applies to classes as well.

Many start thinking that they are going to only put their options into equities such as Apple or Google. However, if you're not putting it in other places, it will make your portfolio become too weighted in one area. You should also make sure that it's not overlapping with one another as well, such as if you own both stocks and mutual funds. You should look at the company and what they hold before investing in it, because you might end up investing too much into one area.

The reason why you should watch for this and make sure that you allocate effectively is because the more diverse a portfolio means that there will be less swings or losses when volatility happens. In recent years however, the downturns can be correlated, so make sure that if you're investing, don't put everything into one market. If you put everything in real estate, it can end up ruining you, such as the case of many investors during the 2008 housing bubble burst.

## The Importance of Differences

Options that are diversified actually can make a difference in a portfolio. Options, especially ones that are volatile, can be seen as a class. They can also be used to protect you overall. You can use ETFs to help with this, and it can be helpful when it comes to hedging. Having a different portfolio can help you prevent anything awry from happening, and it can also show that you're in a good positon in case if things go bad.

## Watching Overall Risk Capital

You need to watch out for the overall risk capital. If you're trading options, you should watch for it increasing above 15-20% of the overall risk capital. This is because if you let it exceed, you're putting yourself at risk and you might have too much on the table. You will also need to plan in case if the stop-loss happens to you, you might lose more of your capital than expected. That's why you should make sure that your portfolio only has that much, and if it exceeds act accordingly.

**Watch Option Account**

If you have an option account, you need to watch how much is on the market. You should make sure that no more than 50% is on the market at any time. It's risky to even have 50% on the market, so it might be best to have less than that when you can.

**Watch Singularities**

For a single option, you should make sure that it doesn't represent more than 5% of the options portfolio on the risk side. If that positon starts to fail, it will not hurt you if it's that number. That's because it can usually go down to about 2.5%, which is only a 50% loss. It's better to make sure you don't put too much into one area than to rely on one option to save it all.

## Trade How You're Comfortable

The problem with many beginner traders, is that they don't trade with what they're comfortable with. Many credit products are hard to understand, but the bigger issue at hand is that they are double-leveraged products. Many who are beginning are not comfortable with their construction and behavior. You should make sure that you know how you're working with the product, because if you're not familiar enough with it, you're not going to get anywhere with it. It can save you if you keep this risk management strategy in, and as you combine this with learning, it can make your ability to trade options that much better.

## Manage your Money

Managing money is vital for this. You only have a certain amount to use, so you have to keep control of it in order to prevent it from being lost forever. The best thing to do is to positon-size, which is when you decide how much you want to enter into any options trade. By doing this, you can determine how much you want to invest, and how much of a percentage you will put into something. You should only use a small amount so you're not relying on one outcome. Some trades can turn out bad, but if you manage it right and only put a certain amount into it, you'll be able to decide how much you're going to put in and how bad the possible risks can be.

**Manage Orders**

If you want to manage the risk in a simple, but effective manner, you can use different options order to be placed. Along with the four main order types, you can put in different options orders to help with risk management. You should look at what will help you, and sometimes, this can help prevent you from selling at a less favorable price. There are orders that you can automatic and lock in a profit in order to cut losses. If you use a limit stop order for example, these can control when you exit the position. This will help avoid the scenarios where you miss out on profits through holding a position too long, or it will prevent any big losses because you didn't blackout fast enough.

**Watching options Spreads**

Watching the options spreads can give you a clear indication on how the stock will move. For example, if you bought some calls on a stock and then wrote cheaper out of money calls on the same stock, that ends up being a bull call spread. You should use these spreads to help manage risks. You can reduce the costs of entering a position, along with minimizing how much you want to use, ad this can help limit the overall risk.

These spreads will also help with short positions as well, and as explained earlier, they're all described to you. You can use these to determine when to leave, and even how the trend of the market is going. This can prevent losses from being incurred, and it can save you in the long run. These spreads are important for anyone working on trying to reduce the risks of various options trading, and they're very important to know.

Options trading could seem like a big, complicated affairs, but limiting the options trading risks is how you put yourself into a position where you know what's going to come out of it, and what will come about. Doing so will help minimize the losses and will assist in maximizing the gains you want in your options trading.

# Conclusion

Thank you again for downloading this book!

I hope this book was able to help you.

The next step is to apply what you've learned.

Finally, if you enjoyed this book, please take the time to share your thoughts and post a review on Amazon.   It'd be greatly appreciated!

If you truly received value from this book, then I'd like to ask you a favor.

Would you be kind and courteous enough to leave a good review on Amazon?

Click here to leave a review for amazon.

I aim to reach as many like-minded people as I can with this book. More reviews will help me accomplish that!

Also, if you happen to be a writer or any type of artist as well, you may even have some good karma; your     odds of having more great reviews for your books increases :)

Review the book Here.

P.S. Things change. Trends change. And so will this book. As a token of appreciation for your commitment to downloading this book, enjoy all the free updates to this book version in the future. Take care.

# BONUS: Successful Real Estate Investing

Courtesy of FR Commerce, enjoy a few free chapters of our other books.

If you want to learn more, please visit the Book Page.

### *"Makin' Money with Real Estate"*

### *Increase in property value*

*The value of properties does not always increase and this can be seen during the past few years. These values cannot even beat inflation. For instance you purchased a piece of property worth $500,000 and. You may be able to sell the property for $515,000 after a year when the inflation rate is at 3% but you will notice that that $15,000 profit does not affect your purchasing power since its value is the same as when you purchased it. How is that so? The profit you received was* *not real it was merely enough to cover the inflation rate during that year hence you are not actually $15,000 richer than you were the year before. This kind of situation arises when the government has to make money but it spends more than it has collected in taxes.*

*You must be asking how then do investors make money with their real estate holdings? These investors make money when they take advantage of a situation where in the rate of inflations is predicted to exceed the current rate of long-term debt. You will notice that there are people purchasing properties and they are even willing to take out a loan to purchase those properties. These people are willing to take the risk because they are paying off the mortgage of those purchased properties with dollars which are worth less than their value. This shows a saver becoming a debtor. In fact, a lot of investors made money this way in the 1970s and the early 1980s when the inflation was spiraling out of control.*

### *Rental Income*

*Making money from renting out property is a very lucrative source of income. A great illustration of that would be a game of monopoly. If one has interest in a house, an apartment building, a hotel or an office building then you can rent those out and collect rent in exchange for letting them utilize those buildings.*

*A useful tool in making money from these properties is the capitalization rate. This rate is a special financial ratio in which the value for which the property can be sold is divided by the value in which they earn per year. For instance, your apartment building may be sold for a million dollars and it earns one hundred thousand dollars a year. One million dollars is divided by the hundred thousand dollars which gives us a ratio of 10 percent.*

*Thus, you can expect a 10 percent return on your investment if you purchased said property in cash and without any debt in acquiring it.*

**Business Operations**

*This type of operation involves business activities and special services. For instance, you are the owner of an office building and you may generate income through vending machines placed in the building and for pay parking. You are able to earn income not just by renting your property out but by providing income generating services that are incidental to you renting it out or to a business that you operate.*

***View SUCCESSFUL REAL ESTATE INVESTING on Amazon here***

# BONUS: Successful Stock Investing

Courtesy of FR Commerce, enjoy a few free chapters of our other books.

If you want to learn more, please visit the Book Page.

*"Preview"*

*" The realm of the affluent are well too familiar with the world of stocks. They know where and how to invest their amassed fortunes, only to grow those fortunes even further as their investments grow in value. Also, those same investments continue to pay off the owners somehow - through dividends, interest, gains, and so on.*

*But here's the best news. That skill - successfully investing in stocks - is not limited* to just the affluent. Fortunately, you don't need to have a business degree to earn profits in stocks either.

But first...

Are you willing to learn further?

Are you not afraid to fail?

Do you have the will and focus to move forward? No matter how bad the news and markets blare at you?

If you answered yes to all the above, carry on. (if not, you may wanna return this book. Stocks are NOT for the weak!)

Good. now let's move forward.

The following first few chapters introduce you to the world of stocks. They will give you some background in stocks, so you'll be able to understand how this investment product works and how it can help you build your wealth.

*In the next chapters, by practicing some simple guidelines such as making regular investments in proven companies, risks can be minimized. Adequate knowledge can help you make sound decisions. Hence, the most basic rule in investing is: Know what you're getting into! "*

*__View SUCCESSFUL STOCK INVESTING on Amazon here__*

## " Defining the Stock Market "

## Market Types Explained

*Perhaps you have heard about primary markets and secondary markets and you might have wondered what its relevance to the stock market is. You may have even asked yourself how many stock market types are there...*

### Primary Markets

*On the one hand, securities are created (via IPO – Initial Public Offering) in primary markets. It is basically a market in which companies sell stocks to the public for the first time.*

*When a company decides to go public, a set of requirements has to be fulfilled first.*

*One, an underwriting firm should be contacted to identify the legal and financial details of a public offering.*

*Two, filing of a preliminary registration statement, known as the preliminary prospectus, should be made with the appointed authorities. The statement should detail the company's prospects and interests. Note that this document is neither a solicitation nor is it finalized. It is simply a set of documents that describes the company's intent.*

*Three, the appointed authorities must approve the finalized statement and the final prospectus, the document that details the stock price, benefits, restrictions. It is a legally binding document for the company and its would-be shareholders. In primary markets, the stocks are purchased straight from the issuing company.*

### Secondary Markets

*When people talk about the stock market, they usually refer to the secondary market. It is formally defined as the venue* where investors can trade previously issued securities minus the involvement of the issuing companies.

In the secondary market, investors buy shares from other investors. This is what we commonly recognize as the "stock market". It encompasses the New York Stock Exchange, Nasdaq, and all the other exchanges around the globe. In this case, the issuing company is not involved in any way in the exchange. Investors trade with fellow investors who own the shares that you would like to either buy or sell.

Secondary markets are further subdivided into auction markets and dealer markets:

### Auction Market

A feature of an auction market is that all parties interested to trade securities, either as an individual or institution, assemble in an area and announce their target buying or *selling price - or the bid and ask price. The aim of this system is to bring all parties together until each has found a counterpart offering an agreeable deal.*

### Dealer Market

*In the case of a dealer market, all parties do not have to assemble in a central hub. Market participants are connected via electronic networks. In this system, the dealers have an inventory of securities which they can buy or sell to the market participants. Different dealers offer a spread of prices where they would like to buy or sell the securities. This option gives investors an idea of the best possible price that they can avail in making a trade.*

**View SUCCESSFUL STOCK INVESTING on Amazon here**

# BONUS: Successful Forex Trading

Courtesy of FR Commerce, enjoy a few free chapters of our other books.

If you want to learn more, please visit the Book Page.

### *"Introduction"*

You know how that saying goes, "Money makes the world go round".

Nowadays, for you or anyone to live comfortably, you should have enough money to buy the things you need. Food, shelter, water, a way to get around, everything.

However, a lot of people are currently experiencing that gruelling feeling of living from paycheck to paycheck and they are barely surviving the day. Since their job would probably take most of their hours in a day, there is not much time for them to take on another job. And trust me, a lot of colleague, friends, and myself have been there. It sucks. Period.

There are several options that you can take in order to solve this problem: one is to scrimp on the daily necessities and save up (and invest in time deposits, mutual funds or stocks), and another is to find other ways to make money without hurting your day job. The first one is definitely painful; to do away with enjoying life and its luxuries just to save a meager amount isn't fair. What's the point of saving up if you don't make enough money in the first place? That leaves everyone to resort to the other, better option.

Through foreign exchange trading, you can definitely make money in the comfort of your home and at your own pace. With the advent of technology, trading through the foreign exchange, or forex for short, has become a lot easier; everyone can trade with other people from anywhere in the world.

Forex is definitely advantageous compared to other investment vehicles. In forex, you trade yours or people's money through an online platform to gain a profit. And there is no person in the world who doesn't need money, so there will always be somebody who is willing to buy forex. It's very easy to sell; that's why the profits are instantaneous – no more waiting time needed unlike in other investments such as time deposits and mutual funds.

More importantly, there is an unlimited earning potential in forex. In other financial instruments, such as savings deposit and fixed income securities, the income is already defined by the fund manager. In forex, it is you, the trader, who has the control of the earnings.

This book will teach you how to start trading successfully in forex and make your money work for you - literally.

*View SUCCESSFUL FOREX TRADING on Amazon here*

# Copyright Notice